CULTURE
CHANGE
THROUGH
ENVIRONMENT
CHANGE

Changing the workplace environment through
psychological safety and human centered
leadership

PAUL HYLENSKI

DEDICATION

This is my first book and dedicated to my mother. She is the woman that made me see that anyone can change the world if they have a vision and purpose to.

CONTENTS

ACKNOWLEDGMENTS

Writing a book is never easy. This is my first book. This book comes from a passion and a vision inside of me but also through personal reflection. This book might illustrate how to change a culture, which is drastically needed in most workplaces, but it is a story to make the world better. Most people go to work each day and work in a toxic environment that causes them untold amounts of stress and they inevitably bring that stress and frustration home to their families. As leaders it is our job to make the lives of the people in our charge better. This book illustrates how to change a culture and some personal stories, but not with the purpose solely to be successful or make a business more profitable. The intent of this book is to share the message of human capital and human leadership. Many companies are starting to turn to this now as they realize that the old type of authoritative leadership is not working with the new generation. The secret is that it didn't really work with the old generation. This is a topic I have firsthand knowledge of. As a child I saw the effects of this type of leadership and work environment, in the Marine Corps I saw what good teams could be, and as a business leader, I saw what good and bad leadership will do to morale and engagement. This movement towards human leadership is a passion for me and I have a vision for a better tomorrow and a better world.

Exceptional leaders understand that they are not complete without the teams that follow them. If the leaders can truly lead through human centered leadership, then they will find that people will gravitate toward them and become more engaged.

I have had the honor to work with such people. They have changed my life. In this book I briefly illustrate how working with poor leaders is a truly life changing event, once you work with an exceptional leader. The poor leaders teach us the most. We learn by their mistakes; it is important for us to learn and not continue the cycle of damage.

As leaders we have the great honor of impacting the trajectory of our people. Most of the times people are resistant to any change, even good change. This is the critical and daunting task ahead for leaders. Most people will not accept change until they see it work. This is the hard part ahead of us. Because the journey to culture change takes years. It takes persistence and courage. This book is a collection of strategies put together as a road map for culture change in a workplace. This does not encompass all of the available tools to change a culture, but if you use this road map you will be on the way to creating a better tomorrow through human leadership and psychological safety.

I am truly grateful to the leaders and teams I have had, because it is through their beautiful work that they have inspired me to become a better person and make the world better. In the end, I feel that is what leadership and the power of inspiration is about.

1 DEVELOPING THE PURPOSE

Leadership is an essential part of the Marine Corps. The knowledge and expertise of a leader are invaluable in any situation, but especially in the military. The Marine Corps has a distinct culture and set of values that are designed to ensure success, and leaders must embody these values in order to effectively lead and guide their Marines. The four core values of the Marine Corps are Honor, Courage, Commitment, and Integrity. Marines are expected to lead by example and demonstrate these values. Additionally, Marines must understand the importance of selflessness, sacrifice, and determination to be successful leaders.

The Marine Corps emphasizes that leaders must be willing to sacrifice themselves for their people. This is exemplified in the Marine Corps Core Value of Honor. Honor is defined as "having the moral courage to do what is right and to adhere to a strict moral code of personal integrity." Leaders must have the courage and determination to do what is right and act with integrity, even when it is difficult. This philosophy is exemplified in the Marine Corps' motto: "Semper Fidelis" which translates to "always faithful." This motto emphasizes that Marines must be faithful to their country, their mission, and their people. Marines must be willing to sacrifice themselves for their people in order to accomplish the mission and protect their country.

Despite the Marine Corps' emphasis on leadership, there are countless examples of poor leadership in both the military and the civilian workforce. Poor leadership in the civilian workforce can take many forms and can have a variety of negative impacts on organizations. One of the most common examples of poor leadership is creating a toxic work environment. A toxic work environment is one that is characterized by low morale, a lack of trust and respect, and a general sense of hostility. This type of environment is created when leaders fail to create a productive and positive environment.

Leaders who create toxic work environments often foster a

sense of animosity and competition between employees. This type of environment can lead to a lack of collaboration, a negative attitude towards work, and diminished morale. Moreover, leaders who foster a toxic work environment often do not provide adequate support or resources to their employees, which can lead to feelings of resentment and apathy. Additionally, leaders who create a toxic work environment often fail to provide clear direction or feedback to their employees, resulting in a lack of accountability and a sense of confusion.

As leaders we are the sum of our experiences and the previous leaders that we have had. Great leaders take all the good that they have learned from their previous leaders and institute it and tend to leave most of the bad by the wayside. The fallacy still exists that we believe we are better than our leaders were to us so that it must be a better environment for our people. The fact of the matter is we are still providing a psychologically unsafe environment even though we believe we are doing better than our predecessors. The system is so degraded that even when we think we are improved we are still leading with fear and intimidation. This type of leadership is more prevalent in manufacturing environments. The old-style pension system created a sense of false security for companies. They believe that the people were not leaving because they were happy when in fact, they were not leaving because of the pension that they were accruing. This drove companies to believe that they did not have to focus on their employees, because they felt they false sense of security with low turnover rates and higher retention good as companies started to phase out eventually realized that they were flawed in their thinking.

We have all had bad leaders throughout our journey. I had one such leader. This leader was respected throughout the business, but not because of technical expertise or strategic prowess. His respect came from fear and intimidation. He showed me what people would do when they were being led at the base level. The base level of leadership is where people follow you because you are the "Boss". This leader would constantly lead through fear and intimidation, most of the time publicly. At the time I was working for him I could not see how distorted and damaging his leadership really was. The closest analogy to this I can come up with is that I like to think that I had Stockholm syndrome. I could not see the damage, from the anxiety and poor treatment, that he was doing to myself and all of the people around. He would regularly call us in for meetings and berate us for hours and make no forward progress for what we were meeting for. He would make us stay late for no reason, or a trivial reason, other than to rehash what he had discussed earlier in the day. We could not readily admit our mistakes and he would regularly pit peers against each other so that we were incentivized to report each other to him. There was no teamwork and there was no inclusion. All of my peers hated each other. We found refuge in the few moments in the day that he decided to be kind to us. Like a traveler wandering through the desert who comes upon water, we would wish every day for this event to happen so that we could take a few sips of the kindness we could get. I learned more from his poor leadership and the anxiety that he had created in me than I would have ever learned from any book or manual. I did not want to come to work every single day, when I did go to work, I was not as useful or productive as I could have been. I was not motivated; in fact, I was demotivated every single day. What I did not realize then was giving me one of his gifts that I could have received, he was showing me what the impact was of poor leadership. I was feeling it every single day with my elevated blood pressure, high anxiety, and overall depression. I was watching someone use manipulation, fear, intimidation, and extreme authoritative leadership. Later I would find out I was watching, exactly how not to lead.

When I had an opportunity to be transferred to a different department, I took the opportunity with excitement. I got to work under another leader that had been at the company for quite some time. He had something that the poor leader did not. He was widely renowned as one of the smartest men at the company. He was a technical expert. He would have had all the ability to lead poorly and still rely on his technical expertise, but instead he was one of the most transformational leaders that I have ever worked for. I must preface this with my Marine Corps service. I have served with great leaders, and I have served with poor leaders. In my military life I learned that leadership does not start and end with the professional part of the job. When you lead someone, you must be willing to care about them. This is where authentic leadership comes into play. People can tell when you care about them and when you are just acting. As a Marine you oversee other Marines. You must be cognizant of everything as a leader. Your life will depend on the emotional and physical well-being of the marine next to you. This teaches you as a leader to care about the entire human. This is where I started my human centric journey.

Once I was transferred at the company, I met the most transformational leader that I have ever met. He had all of the reasons to be a poor leader in this toxic environment and still would have succeeded due to his technical expertise. Instead of being cold and transactional he was the most caring person out of all the leadership team. He spent time with people that no one else would invest in, he cared about people in a way that I had never seen before, and it translated to people working harder and more efficiently for him than anyone. He normalized mistakes and made it to where people were not afraid to tell the truth or to tell the misses. Through this communication and transparency, growth and improvement happened. Innovation flourished because people were telling the truth improving the process. This leader honestly cared about the people in his charge. He would often call just to check in, he would make time to listen to people. He taught complex subjects and made them easy to understand. When people would make mistakes, he used it as a growth opportunity instead of a chastising session. He frequently asked for feedback on how he was doing or if he had been outside of himself going to meet. When he made a mistake, overreacts to a situation or does anything that was contrary to the culture change he would promptly apologize. This taught me that it was acceptable to make mistakes as a leader and that if I did make a mistake to promptly admit my mistake. Through me following his leadership style, the people that were in my charge learned that they were safe if they made a mistake as long as they admitted their mistake. In this type of environment, he showed me how psychological safety could reshape people, he didn't know that he was doing it, but he changed me as a person. I felt safe for the first time at work, and it showed. I wanted to come to work instead of having to, the level of quality of my work skyrocketed and I was instantly recognized for outstanding performance. Most people attributed this to my work ethic, but it was due to this leader providing me with psychological safety. He is the reason for this book, and he is the reason that I have proof that this works. What I was seeing was leadership being done on level two and three. The advanced levels are when people will work and perform not because you are the "Boss", but because they want to work for you, and they believe in your vision. I believed in this man, his vision, and who he was. This was the most transformative thing to happen to me and is in large part why I am on the journey I am today.

Leadership, at its very core, is serving people. Most leaders do not realize the power that they have and changing the trajectory of their people's lives. It is a solemn responsibility.

2 THE POWER OF VISION AND PURPOSE

Samuel Pierpont Langley was an American astronomer, physicist, inventor, and aviation pioneer. He is best known for inventing the bolometer, a device that measures the intensity of infrared radiation, and for his pioneering work in aeronautics, which included developing the first powered, heavier-than-air flying machine.

The life and work of Samuel Pierpont Langley are a fascinating example of the sometimes very different paths that visionary individuals can take. Langley was born in Roxbury, Massachusetts in 1834, and grew up during an age when scientific knowledge and exploration was rapidly increasing. He was an avid student of mathematics and physics and earned an undergraduate degree from the Boston Latin School and a doctorate from Harvard University.

Throughout his career, Langley was driven by his ambition to be famous. He coveted and strove for the recognition that came with scientific success. His ambition was so strong that it sometimes overshadowed his scientific research, leading him to pursue projects that seemed more likely to gain public attention, rather than those that were more likely to lead to scientific breakthroughs.

Langley was also driven by a desire for financial success. He wanted to use his scientific skills to make money, and to this end, he pursued projects that could potentially yield large profits. For example, in 1892, he began to develop a revolutionary new type of steam engine, which, if successful, could have brought in a sizable fortune.

In the years leading up to the turn of the twentieth century, Langley devoted much of his time to the study of aeronautics. He was convinced that powered, heavier-than-air flight was possible and he wanted to be the first to accomplish it. As a result, he threw himself into the study of flight mechanics and the design of aircraft.

But Langley's approach to designing aircraft was

fundamentally different from that of the Wright brothers. The Wright brothers had a vision of improving the lives of people around the world by making air travel a practical reality. They saw their work as a way of changing the world. Langley, on the other hand, saw flight as a way of gaining fame and fortune. He was more interested in the potential rewards of being the first to achieve powered flight than in its wider implications.

This difference in approach was ultimately the Wright brothers' undoing. Langley was more focused on the technical aspects of aircraft design, while the Wright brothers placed more emphasis on experimentation and testing. As a result, while Langley was able to construct a number of powered aircraft that were able to fly short distances, none of them were able to achieve sustained, controlled flight.

Ultimately, Langley's ambition and drive for financial success led to his downfall. While the Wright brothers' vision and dedication enabled them to achieve their goal, Langley's ambition and desire for fame and fortune caused him to take shortcuts and focus too much on the potential rewards of flight. As a result, he was never able to achieve his life's ambition of being the first to fly.

The life and work of Samuel Pierpont Langley provide an interesting case study in the different paths that visionary individuals can take. While Langley was undoubtedly ambitious, his ambition was ultimately his undoing. The Wright brothers, on the other hand, had a clear vision of transforming the world through the power of flight and applied themselves diligently to the task at hand. It was this focus that ultimately enabled them to achieve their goal and revolutionize the world.

Vision and Purpose are fuels that drive change and innovation. Vision and purpose fuel innovation in ways that an abundance of resources cannot. My vision and purpose for a better world in manufacturing started when I was a child. My father worked for a large aerospace company and was constantly frustrated, disengaged, and unappreciated for his efforts. He was frequently subject to layoffs and faced incredible financial instability and hardships which increased his frustration levels and eventually that resulted in his spreading this frustration with the family. This is common in the industry. Marital and family issues are very prevalent in the industry and one of the main factors of this is the way the workforce is treated. They inevitably take this frustration home to their families. I didn't know it then, but what I was watching and experiencing was the effects of the toxic style environment of a profit centric leadership. This style of leadership is riddled with authoritative and micromanaging managers that disengage the worker population.

The mathematical equation $B = f(P, E)$ is simple enough at its roots, but this equation can change Aerospace Manufacturing and even quite possibly the world. Kurt Lewin is considered one of the fathers of modern-day sociology and is the designer of the equation. The most interesting part of his equation is that this was derived back in the 1930's. The answer has been in front of us for all these years and people are just now starting to listen. If we change the environments that we work in, we can change the behavior of our teams without even effort. This equation is paramount to how to change the aerospace manufacturing culture and even the way we do business at all.

As employee loyalty started to decline due to the elimination of pensions and other company provided benefits, leadership started to switch to an authoritative and "prison style" leadership to control costs. This resulted in a fear-based environment where employees felt they had no voice and were not psychologically safe. These types of environments brought an increase in quality defects, workplace injuries, and a reduction in employee engagement and satisfaction.

Psychological safety is a term that, up until recently, has scared leadership, especially in the manufacturing sector. Most business leaders assumed that this would mean a reduction in accountability or that they would have to always result to being "nice". Environments of the past were high accountability and had historically low psychological safety. This produced a toxic and potentially volatile environment in which people are incentivized to hide the truth and are not permitted to make mistakes and contribute. Environments with low accountability and low psychological safety die out because they do not perform, and they do not improve. The optimal environment is high accountability and high psychological safety. This environment provides standard work, operational rigor, and the ability to make mistakes and learn from them. People in these types of environments feel free to improve their skills, contribute to the team with ideas and innovations, and even challenge their leadership when they see issues. This is optimal and out of reach for most companies unless they are prepared to radically change.

3 TOXIC CULTURES AND THEIR ORIGINS

The impacts of poor work environments can be far-reaching and can have significant consequences for organizations. Poor work environments can lead to a decrease in productivity and a decrease in employee engagement. When employees are in a toxic work environment, they are more likely to feel unmotivated and uninspired. This can lead to a decrease in productivity and a lack of innovation and creativity.

Furthermore, poor work environments can have a negative impact on employee morale. Employees in a toxic work environment are often disengaged, apathetic, and lacking in motivation. This can lead to a decrease in job satisfaction and a decrease in overall morale. Moreover, employees in a toxic work environment are more likely to be stressed and anxious, which can lead to an increase in absenteeism and turnover.

Poor work environments can also have a negative impact on organizational performance. Poorly managed and toxic work environments can lead to a decrease in quality and a decrease in organizational performance. Employees in a toxic work environment are less likely to adhere to organizational policies and procedures, which can lead to mistakes and errors. Furthermore, poor work environments can lead to a decrease in customer satisfaction as employees may be less likely to provide proper customer service and support.

From the early days of American industrialization workers have had to endure with poor leadership. Of course, there are pockets of good leadership within history, but the growth of manufacturing and business has always focused on profit and not the people. From early Titans of industry such as Ford, Carnegie, and Rockefeller, the American worker has been used as a tool for profit rather than an asset. In all of these industries the workers were the most important part of the company. Regrettably, companies did not treat these people like that. Companies treated the workers like they were dispensable and started a work environment that was authoritative and had poor conditions. At this time in history, jobs were scarce, so workers did not leave. They endured these horrible conditions because they had to. The poor treatment of workers culminated in the advent of the unions. Workers needed to feel as if they were supported. The unions formed and gave the workers a feeling of inclusiveness and protection. reform came because of a result of the unions. Companies soon realized that the strength of the company was in the workers. They could not make a profit; they could not function without the people doing their jobs. This was the union's greatest leverage. Companies change the way they interact and treat the employees not because they wanted to but because they had to.

Fast forward all the way to the 1980s. Most work environments and especially the manufacturing environment became very toxic. The leadership style of fear and intimidation had permeated its way through all the industry. There are toxic environments in all industries, but the manufacturing one had become to the point of no return. This toxic environment only emboldened the "Us vs. Them" model that the modern-day union uses to provide an inclusive culture within its members. The unions give a sense of belonging and cohesiveness to the members unlike that of which modern day companies could. There was more access to the leaders of the union and due to its tiered system of representation, there was always someone available to hear any issues or grievances. This provided a system of active listening unlike the company structures that had a front-line leader who was aggressive and intimidating and most of the time had more people assigned than possible to connect to. As leaders, it is possible to change the status quo, but it takes courage to break free from the norms. Change is particularly hard and especially the change required to rewrite a culture within an organization. Our past does not always determine our future. In this book you will see many strategies and opportunities to change the culture. This is by no means the only strategy. This is only meant as a guide for the leaders who have the courage, but do not have a roadmap on how to change or what to change.

The change will be difficult and most likely met with resistance, but it will be so worth it, because in the end, you will reshape your organization, but also make the lives of your people far more enjoyable and for this you will receive endless amounts of engagement. We have a chance to change the past and rewrite the story of leadership forever.

4 PSYCHOLOGICAL SAFETY – WHAT IS IT?

Psychological safety is a concept that has gained increasing focus in the organizational world. It has been defined as the shared belief among team members that they can take risks, express themselves, and be free from the fear of judgment, failure, and retribution (Edmondson, 1999). It is a critical component of successful team performance, enabling teams to collaborate and innovate. Organizations that have implemented psychological safety have reported improved team performance, decreased absenteeism, and reduced turnover.

The concept of psychological safety is rooted in the idea of social acceptance and support. It is about creating an environment where people feel secure enough to be vulnerable, exchange ideas, and take risks without fear of judgement or retribution. This requires a culture of openness, respect, and trust. This paper will explore the ways in which organizations can create and promote psychological safety in the workplace.

Specifically, it will discuss ways to generate more inclusive safety, reinforce learner safety, and incentivize contribution safety.

Psychological safety in a work environment has four basic levels. Think of these levels as a triangle. Each level is built on top of the previous. Inclusive safety is at the base level. Developing a feeling of safety and inclusion in teams is the foundation for building an environment of engagement. At this level, it is critical to utilize the human need to feel included and as a part of a team or family. With numbers and community, internal feelings of safety develop. Once this level is reached in an organization the teams start to interact with empathy and pride in their departments. Exceptional leaders can do this on a larger scale. It is hugely impactful to have a common vision and clear goals to unite multiple departments under one organization.

The second level is feeling safe to learn. Learning anything new is, at its very core, stressful. No one wants to feel that they are inadequate or unknowledgeable. It is uncomfortable to learn new things. Group learning environments make this easier and less stressful. The best way to cultivate this is through developing structured learning environments. One of the best ways to cultivate teams and relationships is through structured meeting times and bringing the team together at regular intervals to learn. Training should emphasize learning from mistakes and the ability to freely interact without fear of embarrassment or making mistakes. Learning is more efficiently cultivated by utilizing the adult learning cycle and catering the learning environment to the style preferred to most of the team. Surveys and team sensing sessions are a great way to identify what types of media the team will respond best to. Additionally important is the way the leader conducts the training. Team learning is a great way to reinforce psychological safety while also building the image of technical expertise in the leader. This is important because if the team feels the leader knows the job and can have compassion while teaching it, they will begin to feel safe to ask questions that arise outside of the training and thusly improving the rapport between leader and learner. Psychological safety builds at this level.

The third level of psychological safety is the ability to freely contribute. This is a critical piece that most companies get wrong or don't fully capitalize on. The biggest asset to a company is the people and the ideas within the company. There are many examples of this done well at companies. Only a few good examples exist in manufacturing. Barry Wehmiller is one of the best examples for how to do this right. Their CEO Bob Chapman is a visionary and has inspired great leaders in this field such as Simon Sinek. This is a beacon of hope and they have forged a portion of the roadmap to change aerospace manufacturing. Another great example of empowering contributions from employees is the company Pixar. They attribute a large portion of their success to their passion for creating a horizontal hierarchy and a safe environment to contribute and share ideas. Leaders must incentivize and empower teams as they lead group meetings. Each interaction where an idea is shared with a leader is an opportunity for the leader to increase or decrease the psychological safety of an organization at this level. There are very few examples of this done correctly in aerospace management. Too many poor examples exist. The need to change this is paramount. In aerospace there is less forgiveness for defects and unengaged workforces. The industry has built quality walls in these environments with redundant inspections to provide safety to the consumers, but the answer is simpler. Create an environment where people feel safe to share ideas and build innovation.

The fourth and most important level is the safety to challenge. This is where employees feel safe to challenge decisions by their leaders, challenge existing processes, and to challenge any ideas perceived as poor decisions. Leaders cannot know everything and most of the times there will be blindsides to the leader. By cultivating an environment where the teams and employees feel safe to respectfully challenge their leadership, there is collaboration to ensure that the business and leader see all potential sides and effects of issues and decisions. This gives the leadership and organization a better chance to make good sound decisions. Engaging teams to help and inviting them to provide feedback in business strategy or decisions provides more empowerment to make the decisions successful. The team is bound together because they all had opportunities to provide feedback.

All the levels of psychological safety do one incredibly important thing as the organization climbs through the different levels. It changes the environment that exists in the business. As Kurt Lewin stated, if an organization can change the environment, they can change the behavior of the people within the organization. Employees become more engaged in solutions where they feel safe to make mistakes. They focus on the solutions rather than protecting themselves from retaliation to the mistake. In this environment, leadership can focus on fixing the real problems and the teams are more engaged in helping the efforts. Blindsides in leadership decisions can be caught earlier and free discussion and learning can occur in these types of environments that are rich in psychological safety.

The roadmap to changing an environment, particularly in manufacturing is extremely difficult, but is also very achievable. Kurt Lewin gave us the mathematical equation for how to do this back in 1938. The equation is the basis for proving human leadership is the key and the path forward to better manufacturing and a better world. Amy Edmondson gave us the framework and ideas of psychological safety, so that we can drive to improved metrics and engagement. Edward Deming gave us the framework to improve quality and decision making, but more importantly drove the importance of safety to stop when issues arise and fix the problem. He tried this in American manufacturing plants but was met with resistance and skepticism. He left for Japan and met a receptive audience at Toyota. He and his processes are credited with being the reason why in the 1980's a Toyota Corolla had a higher quality rating than a Rolls Royce vehicle.

Everett Rogers' Law of diffusion of innovations gives us

another roadmap for how to truly change the culture. Most companies look at culture change as a marketing campaign or something that is the "flavor of the month". This is the wrong approach and is most likely why these initiatives are not sustainable. If we, as leaders, use the Law of diffusion, we can use surveys and polls in our work environment to see the current situation. The law of diffusion, summed up, states that in any group of people they always follow a standard deviation. A leader can always expect about 15% of the organization to be bought in to whatever they change. This population are considered the "innovators" and "early adopters" in an organization. About 16% are considered "laggards" and are always the last to adopt change or innovation. The middle group of people are considered "early majority" and "late majority". They will only get onboard to a change or innovation when they see results or sustained efforts. True culture shift or market infusion happens when about 25% of the population start to conform or believe in the change. The standard bell curve then starts to look like a tidal wave. This is a critical tipping point because the wave continues to grow at this point if leaders keep building the system. This is easily tested by regular surveys at intervals or after changes. Leaders need to understand that not all actions are going to be successful. Just like it is important to normalize mistakes and learning in the organization, leaders need to do the same to themselves. If a change does not work, then pivot and make another. Keep changing, keep evolving.

Humans are hard wired to love routine and rigor. People feel safe when they have habits and even if the change is positive, it is hard to adapt. True culture change is extremely hard and sometimes takes a leap of faith. Leaders need to understand they are trying to reprogram an entire environment. It is critical for true change agents to realize that people will be resistant to change at all levels of an organization. It takes courage. Courage to keep going, even when people are skeptics and resistant, and even when some believe you will fail. This is true leadership. Always believe in people. The people are the strength of an organization. They are the organization. Its not the building, the business, or even the leaders. The people are the key. If a leader truly tries, the teams will see, the culture will improve, it will not be overnight, but it will happen. Aerospace Manufacturing is in desperate need of change. For the safety of the millions that fly each year, but also for the millions of families that are impacted daily by the toxic environments. Human capital is paramount, and it all goes back to the simple equation that has existed for over 90 years. Behavior is a function of People and Environment. Have the courage to change the environment and you can change the world.

5 FEEDBACK – WHERE THE JOURNEY STARTS

Culture is an ecosystem. Workplace culture is even more of a fluid ecosystem. We, as leaders, have such a critical role to play in the ecosystem. We control the environment that the ecosystem grows or dies in. How do leaders start? I think this is the scariest part of the journey. The beginning and the end of any journey is the scariest, but also the most important. I think our journey of these articles should start here. The beginning of the journey.....

"A journey of a thousand miles begins with a single step." – Chinese Proverb. How does a leader begin to change a culture. John Maxwells states in his book the 21 Irrefutable Laws of Leadership that the law of Process begins with a Vision, then the framework to the vision, then a plan to achieve the vision. (Maxwell, J. C. (2007)

Culture change is much like this process. It's important to note that the very first step in changing a culture is knowing what and how bad the current culture is. Culture is not a concrete or visible asset. It is the feelings and customs of the people in the environment. The behaviors of the people when they are in the ecosystem. Have you ever noticed that you act in a certain way at work, but when you are home with your family you may be different. This is due in large part to the change in the environment. In different environments, there are different cultures. This point is the starting pole for every culture change. Realizing that you must change the physical and emotional environment in a workplace to change the culture is the basic starting point. Kurt Lewin had the answer all the way back in 1936 when he coined the equation $B = f(P, E)$. Behavior is a function of the Person and Environment. This is great news to leaders. If you can change the environment, then you can change the behavior. Why isn't every company perfect then? Fear of change and fear of the unknown.

How do leaders find out how bad their cultures are? Feedback is the most critical aspect. Most leaders, especially in toxic environments, do a great job of giving feedback, but not of accepting feedback. This creates an environment of fear and lack of psychological safety. Surveys are fantastic tools to get a true sense of the environment. There must be tempered expectations when administering them, especially at the beginning of the journey. Additionally, a good tactic is to utilize the Law of diffusion of Innovations to test the survey for validity and bias. The Law of Diffusion of Innovations gives leaders a roadmap to interpret the data in surveys or feedback to determine if it is biased or follows the normal distribution of populations. The data should follow a normal distribution type bell curve with certain populations in each sector. (Rogers Everett, M. (1995))

If the curve is distorted in either the positive or negative regions, then leaders can see the statistical shift and should act accordingly. This will be critical to understand as we start the change to solicit feedback and properly reacting to the feedback. Knowing how to interpret this and how to react will start to build the blocks of foundation that will later be used to build the house of change.

At the beginning of a culture change when surveys are used, low participation is to be expected. Most people believe that leadership won't listen, don't care, or will retaliate for poor answers. Again, this is normal and to be expected. Do not get discouraged. Culture change is a marathon and not a sprint. Leaders must reinforce by survey design, communication, and survey access that this is an anonymous survey and feedback of any kind is wanted. Good, bad, and ugly. Leaders cannot truly change the environment unless they know what the environment looks like through the perception of the people in it.

Once the data comes in, the most critical step begins. As stated above, the data must be analyzed to determine statistical significance first. In the next article, we will review the process of creating a survey and how to use primer questions to determine the statistical validity of the survey. For the purpose of this article, we will assume that the survey follows the standard deviation on the primer questions. When this occurs, it validates the validity of the survey and shows that you captured the total distribution of the workforce. Once that part is validated, then the work can continue. Each question should be reviewed for statistical shift away from the normal distribution. If it is skewed positively, then it shows acceptance or a positive view on the topic of the question. If it is skewed negatively then the inverse is true. All the negatively shifted questions should be reviewed with the leadership team. You are now starting to interpret the feedback of your people. You are listening, but an important fact here is the teams don't know you are listening yet. If you yell into the woods while you are hiking and hear nothing in return, you assume no one is listening or out there. They have just yelled in the woods, now is your time to let them know they were heard, and you are coming their way to help them.

There will be questions where we cannot understand why the teams answered the way they did. For these questions, propose sensing sessions or a follow-up survey in which more pointed questions about these topics can be asked. As leaders are sensing the environment through surveys for culture, they should also sense how the teams view their leaders or leader. A leadership survey being done in conjunction with a survey of the culture is critical. If people view their leader as not willing to change, they will view the environment the same. Taking feedback for both the leader and environment will start to show a willingness to listen and accept feedback, not just give it. Be ready, this will not be easy and some of the feedback will be hurtful and there will be resistance. Interpret the results in the same fashion as you did the other surveys, using the Law of Diffusion of Innovations. Leaders can see how their teams perceive them and, if they are open to change, can develop an action plan.

That is the biggest deliverable of all of this. All throughout the culture change and maintenance of that culture, getting feedback will be critical to evolving and sustaining the change. Feedback and truly seeing the perceptions of the team is the start. More and more people will take the surveys, each time you do them, if you are communicating results and actions plans correctly. The normal distributions will start to look like tidal waves. Sometimes the truth is hard to hear and even harder to see in writing. It's important to not respond with a defensive posture. That will defeat the entire initiative and effort. Fight the urge!

Once you receive and interpret the information Analyze the results under the spectrum of statistical shifts, then develop an action plan with your leadership teams. Communicate the results to the entire group in a public forum and on multiple platforms. This is their voice and we, as leaders, should be proud that our people are willing to talk to us, even if the information isn't always favorable to us or in line with our perceptions. Explain the results and how you, as the leader, interpret them. It is useful to explain the normal distribution so that the group sees how diverse the opinions are. Then, most importantly, establish and communicate the action plan for everyone to see. This is so vital, because most of the subsequent messaging will follow this platform and should follow your initial action plan. Further surveys and feedback sessions should be tested to see if the "needle" is trending in the right direction.

There are multiple free survey platforms to do this on. There are other ways to do this sensing as well. We must make it safe for the teams to provide feedback to us as leaders. Throughout all these articles, we will be attempting to change the environment. Through little, but effective steps. As Lewin stated in his basic equation $B=f(P,E)$. Behavior is and always be a function of the People and their environment. Very rarely can leaders change people at the very core of who they are, but we have the largest potential impact on the environment they work and stay in. Change the environment and you can change everything. It all starts with simple and easy steps.

6 DESIGNING AN EFFECTIVE FEEDBACK SURVEY

The question is asked frequently. How do I start to change the culture of my organization or team? The answer is very complex and will not be a short journey. The beginning and end of a journey are the parts that come with so much anxiety and apprehension. The truth of the matter is that the answer is within the team or organization. When I say that it is within the team that is to say that they feel it and they know what the culture feels like. Leaders just must find a way to listen to them, and sometimes they don't always want to talk or are afraid to talk because of the culture.

Modern day technology has made this an easier task than it once was. Leaders have a host of survey and polling websites and applications that they can start to sense the environment. This is not easy, and no leader should assume that they are going to get everyone's opinions or that the feedback will be easy to listen to. It will be uncomfortable; you will not get full participation in the beginning. Consistency, Communication and Clarity will be required at this stage.

Surveys and polls come in multiple fashions and designs, but the basic information, design, and analysis of information should follow a close consistent process. Leaders should put creativity, thought, and try to tailor the design and content as best that they can for their organization. The below steps are just a guide. The purpose of these writings is to give leaders a better understand of a basic roadmap for culture change and implementing human centric leadership and psychological safety into their teams and organizations.

In Six Sigma the data is viewed from a very scientific and analytical process, you will notice that some of the suggestions and strategies articulated loosely follow the DMAIC problem solving process of Six Sigma. Analyzing statistics and quantitative data is a science, but I have attempted to break this down, so you do not have to be a statistics-oriented person. While proceeding through this process it is important to view this from an analytical lens.

As brought up before, a particular tool for analyzing this data is the "Law of Diffusion of Innovation". The Law of Diffusion of Innovations helps to interpret the data in surveys or feedback to determine if it is biased or follows the normal distribution of populations. Most groups of populations follow the same standard distribution. Rogers states that there is a tipping point where the distribution gets to a point of mass adoption. During culture change, most leaders attempt to sway most of their workforce. Rogers attempts to lay out another strategy. He suggests first attempting to persuade the higher functioning people in the team. They are easier to persuade and will create a following of the idea that the Early Majority will start to adopt and then the curve will start to look like a tidal wave. The data should follow a normal distribution type bell curve with certain populations in each sector. (See Figure 1). (Rogers Everett, M. (1995))

Step 1: Determine the Information you wish to Analyze

The first step, much like in Six Sigma, is to define what information you want to analyze. What is meant by this is what are you looking to improve or gauge the performance of. This could be a leader, a policy, or even the overall culture. It is important to structure the survey to always go back to the true goal of the survey. A lot of surveys dance around a broad subject and then it makes this more difficult to analyze and implement an action plan later. Another important aspect to think of when designing a survey for your task is to identify any assumptions you may have that you want to test. If you think you need to improve on communication, ask the survey respondents to rank you on Communication, but be more specific so you can develop an action plan to improve. Instead of asking just for communication (which is very broad), maybe ask for ranking on communication of policy, communication of changes in the organization, or communication from the leader. By specifically targeting out the questions, you may find you need to do further research or surveys, but this will give you a good base to launch actions from.

For more participation, a large campaign should be made about the anonymity of the survey. There shouldn't be places to put specific ID numbers of employees or names. This, no matter how it is spun, indicates to the employees that this data is not anonymous. The entire point of a survey is to make the people taking it feel safe to provide real information and candor that they would not say face to face. The more anonymous the survey, the more respondents.

Step 2: Design Survey "Primer" questions

A successful survey, analytically speaking, is a valid survey. How do leaders tell if the survey is valid? What is validity in a survey? Both of those fall in the distribution curve of the Law of Diffusion. The population answering the survey should fall in this curve. Primer questions at the beginning of the survey are critical to see where this distribution of the population is. If you rely purely on questions about performance or culture the answers may be skewed because you are positive or negative in those regions. Primer questions are ambiguous questions meant to test the population in the survey. They are questions that everyone knows the answer to, but you gauge the "temperature" of the survey respondents. Some examples of good primer questions are "Does the leader care about safety?" "How would you rate the company on Quality?". These questions are good at seeing the temperature of the survey. These types of questions are particularly useful. Almost all companies in the world say publicly that their priorities are quality of product and safety of their employees. It is a known fact in the organization, but you can see from the results of the questions what the distribution of the population is. Primer questions should be set up at the very beginning of the survey and requested to be answered in a 1-10 format. This way statistically you can put the data into a histogram and see how this follows the normal distribution of the Law of Diffusion. The scale should be used for some of the key questions in the survey.

At every point in the survey, it should be viewed as a statistical test.   We are scientifically trying to show whether we are positively or negatively shifted away from the standard distribution of the Law of Diffusion.   Used properly, primer questions at the beginning of the survey will tell you if the rest of the survey is valid.   If the primer questions indicate that that survey is shifted positively or negatively, you can expect that the entire survey is shifted in that matter. In this case, the survey can still tell you information, but when analyzing, you should realize that all the data will be biased.   The primer questions can be specific to your environment or organization.

Utilizing the Law of Diffusion can be the difference maker in how you analyze surveys.   Once you realize that around 15-17% of the respondents will most likely have a negative opinion of any question, you can set the stage to see if you are shifted statistically. One thing I have found through my career is that leaders lie, employees lie, sometimes even data can lie, but statistics never lie. With this newfound information setting the stage, organizations can break the old mold of initiatives. The unsuccessful but most widely used way of trying to change anything was through a huge marketing campaign designed to impact the masses. The problem with this issue can only be understood through analyzing the data in the Law of Diffusion.

The Law of Diffusion states that roughly 2.5% of any group are the "Innovators" and these are the highest functioning people within a group. People like Steve Jobs or Elon Musk fit into this group, but in your organization they may look different. You can see these people because they stand out. The next 12.5% of people are considered the "Early Adopters" and they are the people that are change agents. They try to understand the fastest, they also are most likely your top performers in the organization. These could be leaders, or people who "just seem to get it". The next larger batch is the "Early Majority" (34%), and the "Late Majority" (34%). These groups wait to see what the one in front of them are doing and slowly start to move, but only when it is safe or successful. The last Group is the "Laggards" (17%). This is the group that is slowest to adopt change and the most negative of the population. It is important to keep this number in mind when analyzing the data, because a shift in negative responses that is higher than 17% will indicate an area where improvement is needed. (Rogers Everett, M. (1995)

Step 3: Testing the environment issues

When you embark on a survey, you may or may not know what you are actually attempting to fix. This is exactly why you have to spend some time in the "Define" phase of the survey. We have reviewed the primer questions, so now , assuming we have a normal distribution of people in the survey, we can analyze the data collected. So what data do we want to collect? It is important to test the environment for hypothesis'. If you suspect that communication is an issue, phrase a question to be "Rank these items from worst to least", and list some things that you think your organization does well and embed communication in that question. This way you will test your hypothesis. If you don't know where to begin or how the organization feels then ask for one piece of feedback from each employee and then analyze the data into groups. Always request for information that you succeed at and a growth opportunity. This is an important step to test the survey within the survey. If you get nothing but negative remarks on the question "What do we as an organization succeed at or do well?", then you know the survey has had propensity for negativity. Assuming that you have done your work on the primer questions, this can happen in a survey, if you solicit feedback of growth opportunities too frequently. You can subconsciously program the respondents to be more negative in their responses. This is why you have to make it appear as random but solicit feedback that you would perceive as both positive and negative, in some type of alternating way.

It is so critical to test the system, because it is only you perception until statistics and data shows you it is truth. You, as a leader, may think that you are succeeding in an area, but your culture may be so toxic, or worse, you must grow substantially in order to make your teams feel safe enough to tell you the truth. Test assumptions. Test what you think is going well and confirm what you think it not. From all the successful culture surveys in research and ones that I have designed, I think limiting it to no more than 3 negative expected response questions in a row will keep the tone of the survey shifted in the neutral band. This will help you to keep analyzing the questions in the distribution of the primer questions. This is not a constant and will depend on the group and the current culture. The more toxic, the more you will want to alternate.

When doing these surveys, especially in the beginning stages of a culture change, it is important to project an open ear and anonymity. The participants will be scared at first, it is important to reassure them through words and reaction. There should be no reaction to survey, until it is formally published to everyone. The side comments of how the survey is going, or some hard feedback will make people feel as if they cannot say what they want without hurting the leaders' feelings. The purpose of the survey is to improve and listen. Sometimes feedback is hard, but you need to listen and then act as a leader.

Step 4: Analyzing Distribution of respondents on questions

As discussed before, the best way to analyze any of this data would be to put into a histogram and utilize the "Law of Diffusion" to see if your histogram or data is skewed. If using a 1-10 numbering system in the questions , it is easy to see in the percentages of respondents in each section. Putting the data in a histogram can help to see if the data is positively or negatively skewed, or does it follow the normal distribution of the Law of Diffusion. When the distribution is negatively skewed, then it shows statistically that some action is required. Conversely when the distribution appears to be more like a tidal wave towards the positive direction versus a normal distribution it illustrates something is going right.

Multiple choice questions can get you a distribution as well. These questions are some of the most effective to gauge how you are performing on policies, or interactions in the environment. A note of caution, these cannot be Yes/No questions. A successful multiple-choice question would look like "Do you feel as if your front line leader cares about you?".   Then the answers should be written as;

A. A great deal

B. A good deal

C. Neutral

D. Not very much

E. Not at all

By using a 5-answer multiple choice question, you could break this down into a histogram by what percentage of answers you got in each quadrant. For basic assumptions and quick analytics, If you had more than 15% on answer A or E, you could easily see if your data is skewed. You would expect the majority of the answers to fall withing B-D.

Analyzing each question and determining if an action plan is warranted is a huge step and if you are a leader, this should be done with your leadership team that are directly responsible for the teams in the organization.   If you are the front line leader, this should be done with your manager.   You will need to develop an action plan, communicate where the successes are, and project and articulate the change ahead.

Step 5: Determining Action Plans based on data

Now that the data has been collected and analyzed, it is the most important part of the process. You have to somehow articulate that you listened to the feedback, but more importantly is how you are going to react to the feedback. The communication of the feedback should be public and positive. The senior leader should articulate the feedback to the teams. This should include summary data of the feedback and potential action plans for the negative feedback. Showing the teams what the collective group felt, will make them closer and drive more inclusive safety. They are not alone, and the way they feel is more than likely closely aligned with how the group feels. Again, I cannot state the importance of keeping the tone of the feedback review positive. The leader needs to incentivize the behavior which will make the team members who did not take the survey this time, more likely to take the survey next time. A successful review of feedback and action plan will ensure more participation in the next survey. These surveys, reviews, and action plans should be done at least a few times a year. If they are done too frequently, the teams will get "Survey Fatigue", and participation will fall off. If they are not done at all or very sporadically, then people will assume you are not listening or reacting.

7 BE BRAVE – TAKE ACTION

Creating culture change action plans is an essential element in any organization. Organizations depend on successful culture change action plans to create a shared vision and values that will guide the organization through times of change. Creating and communicating a culture change action plan to large groups can be a difficult process. This paper will cover items that should be included in successful culture change action plans, how to effectively communicate them to large groups and how to develop trust through surveys and action plans.

What is a Culture Change Action Plan?

A culture change action plan is a document that outlines the steps needed to improve an organization's culture. It is designed to create an environment that is more diverse, equitable, and inclusive. It identifies specific actions that need to be taken to create an environment where everyone feels safe, accepted, and valued. It also outlines steps to ensure that changes are sustainable and that any challenges can be overcome.

Items to Include in a Successful Culture Change Action Plan (To be discussed with Leadership)

1. Establish a Shared Vision: This is the "Why" and the teams should be reminded of this. This should be at the beginning of the presentation and at the end of the presentation. A shared vision should be established that outlines the organization's goals and values. It should be clear and concise and should be shared and understood by all members.

2. Identify Barriers: An organization should identify the barriers that prevent it from achieving its goals. These might include lack of diversity, inequity, or exclusion.

3. Develop a List of Actions: Once the barriers have been identified, the organization should develop a list of specific actions that need to be taken to address these issues. These should include both short- and long-term goals.

4. Establish a Plan of Action: Once the actions have been identified, the organization should develop a plan of action that

outlines how these actions will be implemented and monitored.

5. Evaluate the Plan: The plan should be evaluated on a regular basis to ensure that it is effective and that any challenges are addressed in a timely manner.

6. Communicate the Plan: Once the plan has been established and evaluated, it is important to communicate it to all members of the organization. This should be done in a clear and concise manner, so that everyone is aware of what is expected of them and how they can contribute to the success of the plan.

Communicating a culture change action plan to large groups can be a challenging task. It is important to ensure that all members of the group are aware of the plan, and that they understand and are committed to its implementation.

Here are some tips for communicating a culture change action plan to large groups:

1. Make sure the language is clear and concise: It is important to ensure that the language used is clear, concise, and easy to understand. This will make it easier for everyone to understand

the plan and to participate in its implementation.

2. Provide regular updates: It is important to keep everyone informed of the progress of the plan. Regular updates should be provided, so that everyone knows how the plan is progressing and how they can contribute to its success.

3. Allow for input: It is important to allow for input from everyone in the group. This will ensure that everyone's ideas and opinions are taken into consideration, and that any challenges can be addressed in a timely manner. If people are willing to add input or clarification during the communication sessions, attempt to positively steer these conversations. This can be hugely impactful and reinforce the positive nature of the movement. Do Not Get Defensive!

4. Involve the team: Involving the team in the planning and implementation of the plan will ensure that everyone is engaged and that the plan is more likely to be successful.

5. Be open and honest: It is important to be open and honest about the plan and its implementation. This will ensure that

everyone is aware of the challenges, and they can work together to overcome them.

Creating a culture change action plan is an important step in improving the culture of an organization. However, it is also important to ensure that the plan is accepted and implemented by all members. One of the best ways to do this is to develop trust through surveys and action plans. By using the survey to determine the best course of action and then communicating results and actions to the results, the teams will feel heard. The leader then needs to be accountable for the action plan and then retest success with periodic surveys.

Surveys are an effective way to identify areas of improvement and to gauge the level of acceptance for a culture change action plan. Surveys should be conducted in a way that allows members of the organization to provide honest and open feedback. This can include anonymous surveys, or surveys that are administered in person or via email. Surveys should cover topics such as:

• Understanding of the plan: Ask members to explain what the plan is, what it aims to accomplish, and how it will be implemented.

• Acceptance of the plan: Ask members how accepting they are of the plan, and any concerns or suggestions they may have.

• How the plan will be implemented: Ask members how they feel the plan should be implemented, and what steps should be taken to ensure its success.

• How the plan can be improved: Ask members how the plan can be improved, and what suggestions they may have.

Performing surveys, then developing actions plans is the cornerstone to starting to shift the standard distribution of any group to a more positive one. Explaining the "Why" of what you are doing is critical to the teams understanding the larger purpose. It is important that they see the vision and plan. A ship out at sea without a route or end destination is just drifting

8 UNDERSTANDING EMPLOYEE DYNAMICS

Employee turnover is one of the most serious problems any organization can face. It is a costly and often overlooked challenge that affects all aspects of a company's operations, from the recruitment and training of new staff to the bottom line of the business. When employees leave, it can leave a company with a smaller and less experienced workforce, which can lead to lower productivity, increased employee stress, and decreased customer satisfaction. It is essential for organizations to understand the causes of employee turnover and to develop strategies to reduce it.

Employee morale is also an important factor in any organization. Low morale can lead to decreased motivation, a negative work environment, and a decrease in overall productivity. It is essential for organizations to understand the factors that contribute to low morale and to develop strategies to improve morale in the workplace.

In addition, employee satisfaction is a key factor in any organization. Employee satisfaction is a measure of how content and fulfilled employees feel in their jobs and is an indicator of their level of engagement and commitment to the organization. It is important for organizations to understand the factors that drive employee satisfaction and to develop strategies to improve it.

Furthermore, it is essential for organizations to create a culture of innovation and collaboration that helps employees to feel supported and appreciated. This can help motivate employees and increase their job satisfaction.

What Causes Employee Turnover?

Employee turnover is the number of employees who leave an organization within a certain period. It is an important measure of employee engagement and satisfaction and can have a significant impact on an organization's bottom line. There are a number of factors that can contribute to employee turnover, including:

• Low wages: Low wages can make it difficult for employees to make ends meet, leading to dissatisfaction and a desire to leave the organization.

• Poor management: Poor management can lead to a lack of communication, a lack of direction, and a lack of support, all of which can lead to a decrease in employee morale and a desire to leave.

• Lack of recognition and rewards: Employees need to be recognized and rewarded for their work in order to stay motivated and satisfied. A lack of recognition and rewards can lead to feelings of being undervalued and a desire to leave.

• Poor working conditions: Poor working conditions, such as overcrowded workspaces or inadequate resources, can lead to a decrease in productivity and a desire to leave.

• Stressful or unfulfilling work: Employees need to feel that the work they are doing is meaningful and challenging in order to stay engaged. Stressful or unfulfilling work can lead to feelings of burnout and a desire to leave.

Strategies for Reducing Employee Turnover

There are a number of strategies organizations can use to reduce employee turnover. These include:

• Developing an attractive compensation and benefits package: Organizations should strive to create a compensation and benefits package that is attractive to potential and existing employees. This should include competitive salaries, generous benefits, and a range of perks and bonuses.

• Improving communication: Communication is essential for maintaining employee morale and engagement. Organizations should strive to create an open and transparent communication culture so that employees feel comfortable expressing their concerns and ideas.

• Improving working conditions: Organizations should strive to create a comfortable and productive working environment for their employees. This could include providing comfortable furniture, adequate resources, and a well-lit workspace.

• Offering career development opportunities: Employees need

to feel that they have opportunities to grow and develop in their careers. Organizations should strive to offer employees a range of training and development opportunities so that they can stay motivated and engaged.

• Recognizing and rewarding employees: Organizations should recognize and reward employee contributions in order to maintain morale and engagement. This could include offering bonuses or other incentives for outstanding performance.

Strategies for Improving Morale in the Workforce

Improving morale in the workforce is essential for maintaining employee engagement and satisfaction. There are a number of strategies organizations can use to improve morale, including:

• Creating a sense of community: Organizations should strive to create a sense of community in the workplace by encouraging collaboration, communication, and mutual respect. This could include hosting team-building activities or encouraging employees to socialize outside of work.

• Celebrating successes: Organizations should strive to

recognize and celebrate employee successes. This could include offering awards or other incentives for outstanding performance.

• Encouraging feedback: Organizations should encourage employees to provide feedback and suggestions so that they feel heard and valued. This could include conducting employee surveys or holding regular meetings with employees.

• Providing support: Organizations should strive to provide employees with the resources and support they need to succeed. This could include offering flexible work schedules or providing employees with the necessary tools and technology.

• Promoting work/life balance: Organizations should promote a healthy work/life balance for their employees by offering flexible work schedules and encouraging employees to take time off when needed.

Strategies for Enhancing Employee Satisfaction

Employee satisfaction is a measure of how content and fulfilled employees feel in their jobs and is an indicator of their level of engagement and commitment to the organization. There are a number of strategies organizations can use to enhance employee satisfaction, including:

• Creating a culture of innovation and collaboration: Organizations should strive to create a culture of innovation and collaboration that encourages employees to think creatively and to work together to solve problems. This could include offering project-based work, encouraging employees to share ideas, and providing resources to help employees develop new skills.

• Offering competitive salaries and benefits: Organizations should strive to offer competitive salaries and benefits packages to attract and retain talented employees. This should include competitive wages, generous benefits, and a range of perks and bonuses.

• Promoting diversity and inclusion: Organizations should strive to create an inclusive environment where all employees feel valued and respected. This could include implementing policies and procedures to promote diversity and providing training and resources on diversity and inclusion.

• Offering career development opportunities: Organizations should strive to offer employees a range of training and development opportunities so that they can stay motivated and engaged. This could include mentoring programs, job rotations, or other learning opportunities.

• Recognizing and rewarding employees: Organizations should recognize and reward employee contributions in order to maintain morale and engagement. This could include offering bonuses or other incentives for outstanding performance.

Whether you decide to follow or implement all or some of these, start with one. Changing the employee's experience and environment will change their behavior. They will become more engaged and more willing to support. We must take care of the people for them to take care of our customers and products. Employee dynamics and the understanding of these issues will help with reshaping our environments.

9 CHANGE LEVEL 1 : INCLUSIVE SAFETY

In today's ever-changing business environment, the need for culture change in workplaces is more important than ever. Companies need to be able to adapt to new markets, technologies, and customer demands in order to stay competitive. In order to do this, they must focus on creating a culture that is open to change and encourages innovation and creativity.

Psychological safety is an important concept in organizational settings and is critical to the success of any team. It is the shared belief among team members that they can take risks, express themselves, and be free from the fear of judgment, failure, and retribution. Organizations can create a psychologically safe environment by generating more inclusive safety, reinforcing learner safety, and incentivizing contribution safety. These strategies involve creating a culture of trust and respect, fostering open communication, providing resources and support, and recognizing and celebrating successes. By implementing these strategies, organizations can create an environment where employees feel secure enough to take risks and contribute to the team's success.

Inclusive safety is an increasingly important concept within the modern workplace. It involves creating a workplace environment that enables, encourages, and supports all employees to be their most effective and engaging selves. An inclusive safety culture not only recognizes and celebrates difference, but also actively works to eliminate barriers and disparities so that everyone – regardless of race, gender, age, sexual orientation, or disability – can feel safe, respected, and supported.

Organizations can generate more inclusive safety by creating an environment of respect and understanding. This includes establishing a culture of inclusivity and belonging. This means that employees should feel valued and respected regardless of their background, beliefs, or differences. Leaders should create a safe space for discussion and dialogue by fostering open communication, encouraging collaboration, and providing emotional support. Additionally, it is important to recognize and celebrate diversity. This can be done by promoting an understanding of different cultures, backgrounds, and viewpoints.

Organizations should also promote an understanding of power dynamics. This involves understanding how power is distributed among team members and how different team members may have different levels of influence and access to resources. Leaders should be aware of how this may impact team dynamics and be mindful of how they can create an equitable environment.

To further promote inclusive safety, organizations should ensure that diversity is reflected in team composition. This includes having a variety of perspectives represented on teams and providing equal opportunity to participate in decision-making. Organizations should also consider providing resources and support to marginalized groups.

Creating an inclusive safety culture is not something that can be accomplished overnight. It requires a holistic approach that involves everyone in the organization.

Leaders have an important role to play in fostering an inclusive environment. They must set the tone by creating an open and supportive environment, and by promoting diversity and inclusion. Leaders should also ensure that policies and procedures are in place to protect all employees, and that they are consistently enforced.

Employees should also take responsibility for creating an inclusive safety culture. They should be mindful of their words and actions and be respectful and supportive of one another. They should also be willing to speak up if they feel something is wrong or if they have a different perspective. Creating this environment change is critical to starting a culture chang

10 CHANGE LEVEL 2 : LEARNER/CONTRIBUTOR SAFETY

Psychological safety is an important concept in organizational settings and is critical to the success of any team. It is the shared belief among team members that they can take risks, express themselves, and be free from the fear of judgment, failure, and retribution. Organizations can create a psychologically safe environment by generating more inclusive safety, reinforcing learner safety, and incentivizing contribution safety. These strategies involve creating a culture of trust and respect, fostering open communication, providing resources and support, and recognizing and celebrating successes. By implementing these strategies, organizations can create an environment where employees feel secure enough to take risks and contribute to the team's success.

Organizations can reinforce learner safety by creating an environment that is conducive to learning and growth. This involves creating an environment where employees feel comfortable expressing their ideas and taking risks without fear of judgement or retribution.

To create such an environment, leaders should foster open communication, encourage collaboration, and provide emotional support. They should create an environment where questions can be asked without fear of judgement and where opinions are encouraged and respected. Leaders should also provide clear and timely feedback on tasks and assignments.

Organizations should also provide resources and support to employees to help them grow, develop, and become more effective in their roles. This includes offering training, mentorship, and education opportunities. Additionally, organizations should provide employees with the necessary resources, such as technology and tools, to enable them to be successful.

Finally, organizations should ensure that employees have a clear understanding of their roles and responsibilities. This includes providing employees with clear expectations, objectives, and goals. This helps employees stay on track and ensure that they are working towards the same goals.

Organizations can incentivize contribution safety by rewarding employees who contribute to the team's success. This encourages employees to take risks, express their ideas, and collaborate with others.

Organizations can incentivize contribution safety by providing bonuses to employees who demonstrate high levels of contribution and excellence. These bonuses can be in the form of monetary rewards, recognition, additional time off, or promotions. Additionally, organizations can provide recognition for team performance and success. This can be done through awards, public recognition, or other forms of celebration.

Organizations should also provide employees with opportunities to contribute and be creative. This can be done through hackathons, design thinking sessions, or other forms of collaborative problem solving. Additionally, organizations should provide employees with the resources they need to be successful, such as technology, data, and tools.

Finally, organizations should provide feedback in a constructive and supportive manner. This includes recognizing and celebrating successes, as well as providing constructive feedback when needed. This helps employees understand where they need to improve and how they can become more successful.

11 CHANGE LEVEL 3 : CHANGE THE ENVIRONMENT

As stated earlier, Kurt Lewin, who is widely considered to be the founder of modern organizational psychology, had a profound impact on our understanding of how the physical environment affects our behavior. His work in the 1920s and 1930s focused on how to create more efficient, productive workplaces by examining how the environment can be altered to increase employee morale and effectiveness. This is a concept known as "psychological challenge safety," which involves making changes to the environment that can reduce stress and improve psychological safety. In the decades since Lewin's groundbreaking research, this concept has evolved and become increasingly important in the modern workplace.

Today, the idea of changing the environment to increase psychological safety is relevant in a variety of contexts. It can be used to create more inclusive and equitable workplaces, reduce stress and burnout, or even help to develop innovative solutions to complex problems. By understanding how the physical environment can influence behavior, we can create an environment that encourages creativity and encourages employees to take risks. This is important not just for individual employees, but also for organizations. By creating an environment that encourages risk-taking and creativity, organizations can foster a culture of innovation and make more informed decisions.

Kurt Lewin's concept of psychological challenge safety can be applied in the modern workplace. If, we as leaders, can change the environments that we work and our people interact within, then we can change their behaviors. This is the true key to getting our teams to become more engaged and interested in their work.

As a matter of review: In the 1930s, Kurt Lewin began to develop his theory of psychological challenge safety. His research focused on the idea that individuals behave differently in certain environments. He argued that the physical environment could be altered to create an environment that was more conducive to successful behavior. He believed that changing the environment could reduce stress and promote psychological safety.

Lewin's research focused on the idea that a psychologically safe environment could be created by providing individuals with a sense of security and support. He argued that providing individuals with a sense of safety could reduce stress and make it easier for them to take risks and make creative decisions. He also argued that creating a psychologically safe environment could lead to greater efficiency, productivity, and cooperation in the workplace.

Lewin's research also focused on the idea that the physical environment could be changed to encourage creativity and problem-solving. He argued that the physical environment should be designed to reduce distractions and provide individuals with an environment in which they can focus on the task at hand. He also argued that the physical environment should be designed to provide individuals with a sense of security and support.

Creating a psychologically safe environment has several advantages for both individuals and organizations. For individuals, it can help to reduce stress and promote creativity. By creating an environment that is conducive to taking risks and making creative decisions, individuals are more likely to come up with innovative solutions to problems. This can help to improve productivity and efficiency.

For organizations, creating a psychologically safe environment can help to create a culture of collaboration and innovation. When individuals feel secure and supported, they are more likely to take risks and come up with creative solutions. This can help organizations to become more innovative and make better decisions. Additionally, it can help to improve employee morale and create a more enjoyable workplace.

Creating a psychologically safe environment can also benefit organizations in terms of public relations. By creating an environment that is conducive to creative problem-solving, organizations are more likely to be seen as progressive and forward-thinking. This can help to attract customers and increase positive public perception.

Creating a psychologically safe environment is not something that can be achieved overnight. It requires thoughtful consideration and planning. Organizations must consider a variety of factors, including the physical environment, the organizational culture, and the individual needs of employees.

The physical environment should be designed to reduce distractions and promote focus. It should be comfortable and supportive. This can be achieved through the use of colors, furniture, and other elements that create a feeling of safety and security. The physical environment should also be designed to encourage collaboration and creativity. This can be achieved through the use of open spaces, communal areas, and other features that encourage interaction and brainstorming.

Organizations must also create a culture that is conducive to psychological safety. This can be achieved through the use of clear communication, respect for individual differences, and a focus on teamwork and collaboration. Organizations should also ensure that employees feel valued and appreciated. This can be done through recognition programs and other rewards.

Organizations must also consider the individual needs of employees. This can include providing flexible work schedules, offering training and development programs, and providing access to mental health resources. Organizations should also consider how to create an environment that is inclusive and equitable. This can be achieved through the use of diversity and inclusion initiatives.

Although creating a psychologically safe environment can have a number of benefits, there are also potential drawbacks. One potential drawback is that it can lead to a decrease in efficiency. When employees feel too safe, they may become complacent and less productive. Additionally, a psychologically safe environment can lead to increased risk-taking, which can potentially lead to mistakes and poor decisions.

Another potential drawback is that some employees may feel uncomfortable in a psychologically safe environment. Those who are used to an environment that is more hierarchical and authoritarian may feel that a psychologically safe environment eliminates their sense of power and control.

A psychologically safe environment can lead to an oversimplification of the problem-solving process. When employees feel too safe, they may become too comfortable and overlook important details or underestimate the complexity of the problem.

Although there are potential drawbacks to creating a psychologically safe environment, there are also ways to mitigate them. Organizations can ensure that employees are still held accountable and that there are consequences for mistakes. Additionally, organizations can provide employees with the skills and training they need to make informed decisions and understand the complexities of the problems they are facing.

Organizations can also ensure that employees are given the

opportunity to voice their opinions and have their ideas taken seriously. This can help to ensure that problems are not oversimplified and that the problem-solving process is not hindered. Finally, organizations can ensure that employees understand the importance of taking risks and that mistakes are seen as opportunities for learning and growth.

Kurt Lewin's concept of psychological challenge safety has had a profound impact on our understanding of how the physical environment can influence behavior. By creating an environment that encourages creativity, problem solving, and collaboration, organizations can foster a culture of innovation and make more informed decisions. Additionally, creating a psychologically safe environment can have several advantages for both individuals and organizations, such as reducing stress, promoting creativity, and increasing productivity. However, there are potential drawbacks to creating a psychologically safe environment, and organizations must be mindful of these and take steps to mitigate them. By understanding how the physical environment can influence behavior, organizations can create an environment that

encourages creativity and innovation and helps employees to take

risks and make informed decisions.

12 CHANGE LEVEL 4 : OPTIMIZING COMMUNICATION

The ability of a company to navigate culture change through the alteration of its language can be a powerful tool in setting a new tone. Language shapes the way we think and how we view the world, and through thoughtful and deliberate alterations in the words and phrases that constitute a company's dialect, a culture can be molded to better reflect the core values of the company.

The first step in creating a new culture is to define the core values that the organization wishes to promote. Once these values have been established, the next step is to identify the language that will best reflect them. To do so, it is important to consider the way words are used, the context in which they are used, and the impact they have on the overall culture of the organization.

For example, replacing the term "supervisor" with the term "coach" can create a more collaborative and supportive atmosphere. This shift helps to create a culture where employees feel empowered and supported, as opposed to feeling micromanaged and controlled. Additionally, using the term "team" instead of "department" can help to foster a sense of unity, as it implies inclusion and collaboration.

Changing the language of the company culture can also help to create an atmosphere of trust. Words like "respect", "honesty", and "integrity" can help to build a culture where employees feel comfortable expressing their opinions, and where honesty and vulnerability are encouraged.

When considering language changes, it is also important to consider the impact of tone on a company's culture. Using words and phrases that convey positivity and enthusiasm can help to create an atmosphere of energy and collaboration. Additionally, leaders should avoid jargon or buzzwords that can create confusion or seem pretentious.

Language is an incredibly powerful tool, capable of influencing and shaping the attitudes and culture within a company. It is essential that companies are mindful of how they use language when communicating internally and externally. Language has the power to promote positivity and collaboration, or to create confusion and mistrust.

The tone of language should be taken into consideration when making any language changes. Leaders should look for ways to foster an atmosphere of inclusivity, positivity, and enthusiasm. The use of words and phrases that convey friendliness and optimism can help to create a culture that encourages open communication and collaboration. Additionally, the use of language should be kept simple and straightforward, avoiding the use of jargon or buzzwords that can be confusing or off-putting.

One way to further promote positive language use is to create a "language policy" that outlines the preferred tone for internal and external communication. This document should reflect the company's values, mission, and goals. It can also include specific words and phrases that should be avoided, as well as guidelines for how to handle difficult conversations. By making clear expectations and standards of language use, it will be easier to ensure that everyone is on the same page when it comes to how they communicate with one another.

Leaders should also be mindful of the impact their language can have on their employees. For example, managers should be aware of how their own language use can shape the culture within their teams. Leaders should strive to use language that encourages collaboration, critical thinking, and problem-solving. This can help to create a culture where everyone is comfortable sharing their ideas and speaking up.

Biased or discriminatory language should also be avoided. Companies should be very mindful of how their language can influence the perceptions of their employees, customers, and vendors. Language should be kept professional, respectful, and inclusive. Companies should be proactive in recognizing and addressing language that may be offensive or exclusionary.

It is also important to be conscious of the language used in any advertising or marketing materials. It is essential that companies take into consideration the diverse backgrounds of their customers and audiences and avoid language that can be seen as exclusionary or offensive.

Companies should also consider the impact of language changes on customer service. Companies must ensure that their customer service representatives are equipped with the language and tools they need to communicate effectively with their customers. It is essential that customer service representatives are trained in how to handle difficult conversations and address customer complaints in a respectful manner.

Language can have an incredibly powerful effect on the culture within a company. Companies should take into consideration the impact language changes can have on their employees, customers, and vendors. By choosing language that is positive, respectful, and inclusive, companies can create a culture of collaboration, critical thinking, and problem-solving.

In addition to changing the language of a company culture, leaders should also be conscious of how the physical environment can impact the culture. Introducing physical elements such as plants, art, and music can help to create an atmosphere of positivity and creativity. Establishing an open-door policy, providing comfortable seating, and offering snacks and drinks can also help to foster an atmosphere of inclusivity and collaboration.

Ultimately, by carefully considering language and the physical environment, company leaders can better promote their core values and create a more positive culture. Changing the language of a company culture can help to foster a sense of trust, collaboration, and respect, and can ultimately lead to a happier and more productive workplace.

13 THREE PHASES OF ENVIRONMENT CHANGE

Kurt Lewin was a pioneer in the fields of organizational behavior and social change. He developed a unique three-step process for successful change management, which is still widely used to this day. The three steps—unfreezing, changing, and refreezing—form the foundation of Lewin's change philosophy. This philosophy has been used to help initiate change in many organizations, from small businesses to large corporations, government agencies, and nonprofits.

Kurt Lewin stood in the center of the auditorium, his presence commanding attention from each and every student. His fiery blue eyes seemed to pierce right through them, as if seeking to imprint his message on their souls.

"Let me be clear," he began. "The process of successful change management requires three steps. Unfreezing, changing, and refreezing. This is the basis of my philosophy of change. Unfreezing requires an initial disruption, a jolt to break away from the status quo. Next, we must move on to changing, where adjustments and new approaches are adopted and actual changes begin to take place. Finally, we must move to refreezing, where the changes are stabilized and become the accepted norm."

As he spoke, the students' eyes glittered in anticipation. He had their undivided attention.

"What this process ultimately teaches us," he continued, his voice rising in intensity, "is the importance of taking risks. Without risk, there is no progress, no evolution. It is those brave enough to make the leap who will reap the rewards of a transformed future."

His words hung heavy in the air as he paused for a moment. Then, he continued.

"Without taking a risk, you cannot change. It is only through embracing risk that you can truly unlock your potential and begin to make a true difference."

The students hung on his every word. They were entranced by his passion, his charisma, and his wisdom. His message had clearly moved them.

Kurt Lewin went on to explain how the process of change management applies to organizations. He spoke of how it could be used to implement successful change initiatives in businesses, government agencies, and nonprofits. He emphasized the importance of leadership in making this process successful. He explained that it was the leader's job to lead by example, to take risks, and to be a role model of change.

When his lecture concluded, the auditorium erupted in cheers and applause. Kurt Lewin had communicated his message in a way that had truly resonated with the audience.

As the students filed out of the auditorium, one of them couldn't help but smile. Kurt Lewin had changed his life. Through his words, he had shown the way toward personal and professional growth.

His message had revolutionized the way he viewed change, and it was something he would never forget.

Unfreezing

According to Lewin, the first step in the process of change is to "unfreeze" the current environment. This involves breaking down the existing structure and mindset of an organization in order to create the space for change. Unfreezing is about shifting the current mindset and creating an awareness of the need for change. It requires a lot of self-reflection and hard work on the part of leaders, who must recognize the cultural, political, and organizational barriers that need to be addressed in order to create a successful change effort.

Once the organization is ready to move forward, the leader needs to create a plan that addresses how the organization will move forward. This plan should identify the steps that will be taken to create the desired change. It should also address how the organization will support the change effort and hold itself accountable for the outcomes.

Changing

The second step in the process of change is to actually make the desired changes. This is the most difficult part of the process and requires careful planning, communication, and collaboration in order to ensure that the changes are implemented correctly. This step requires leaders to be proactive and to clearly communicate their vision and expectations. Leaders need to be able to communicate the need for change and their desired outcomes, as well as providing resources and support for the staff to help them make the necessary changes.

Refreezing

The third step in the process of change is to "refreeze" the new environment. This involves reinforcing the changes that have been made and ensuring that the desired results have been achieved. This is a crucial step for organizations to take in order to sustain the changes that have been made. Leaders need to be able to evaluate the effectiveness of the changes and ensure that the new system is working as intended.

Leaders also need to ensure that the positive outcomes of the change are reinforced, and that the organization is adapting to the new environment. This may involve providing additional resources and support to ensure that the desired results are achieved. It may also involve creating new policies and procedures to ensure that the changes are institutionalized.

Kurt Lewin's change philosophy is a proven approach to successful change management. It is based on three key steps: unfreezing, changing, and refreezing. Each of these steps is essential for successful change management and requires the leader to take an active role in ensuring that the desired outcomes are achieved. Unfreezing requires a leader to reflect upon the current environment and the barriers that need to be addressed. Changing requires the leader to develop a plan and to actively communicate and collaborate with staff in order to ensure the desired results are achieved. Refreezing requires the leader to ensure that the new system is working as intended and that the positive outcomes of the change are reinforced. Lewin's philosophy is a valuable tool for any leader who is looking to create successful change in their organization.

14 CREATING HOPE WITHIN AN ORGANIZATION

Leaders have the power to influence the energy and morale of the people in the organization. An effective leader creates an environment of hope, where employees feel supported and motivated to reach their goals. This type of environment inspires people to do their best, reach higher levels of performance, and take on challenging tasks. Creating an environment of hope is essential for the success of any organization.

In my professional career, I have seen the benefits of this firsthand. Early on in my leadership career I was able to build the business from within. Promoting people who were outstanding performers with growth aspirations. At the time there was no avenue to promote these people. Leadership often assumed that because they were in the working population that they were less skilled or motivated. There were a few people that were outstanding performers and could weather the storm of the significant change. These people were given a chance and

CULTURE CHANGE THROUGH ENVIRONMENT CHANGE

invested in. They invested in themselves, and now have reshaped the business for the better. They are the pioneers of the business and what they did was far larger than they most likely imagined they would be able to do. They created a large-scale hope within the organization. This was pivotal for the culture change. They gave every new hire hope that if they did all of the correct things and invested in themselves that they could be more and grow within the company. This is where the HOPE (Helping Others Pursue Excellence) initiative originated. This HOPE initiative drove real hope in growth throughout the organization. This broke down barriers within the organization and was instrumental to some of the changes that would later occur.

Creating an environment of hope in the workplace has many benefits. When there is hope in the organization, employees feel empowered to achieve their goals and they are motivated to do their best. They are inspired to take on challenges, develop new skills, and take risks.

Hope also helps to create a positive culture and a strong team spirit. When everyone is working together towards a common goal, employees feel connected to each other and to the organization. This encourages collaboration, innovation, and creativity.

Hope can also increase productivity. When people are inspired and motivated, they are more likely to put in extra effort and work hard to reach their goals. This has a positive effect on the performance of the organization and can lead to greater success.

Hope can help to reduce stress and anxiety. A hopeful environment can help employees to manage their workloads effectively and it can encourage them to take the time to relax and recharge. This can lead to increased job satisfaction and overall well-being.

Leaders have an important role to play in creating an environment of hope. It is important for leaders to be aware of the power of their words and actions. They should strive to create a culture of positivity and encouragement.

Leaders should also focus on helping employees develop both

personally and professionally. This could involve offering training opportunities, encouraging employees to take on new challenges, and providing feedback and guidance.

Leaders should also focus on creating an environment where failure is seen as an opportunity to learn. This could involve making it safe for employees to try new things and encouraging them to take risks.

Leaders should also focus on creating a workplace that is inclusive and supportive. This could involve providing resources and support to employees from all backgrounds and celebrating diversity.

Creating a culture of hope is essential for any organization. Leaders have the power to create an environment where employees feel supported and are motivated to reach their goals. This can lead to increased engagement, productivity, and overall success. Leaders should focus on providing resources, encouraging employees to take on new challenges, and creating a safe environment where failure is seen as an opportunity to learn.

By creating an environment of hope, leaders can foster a culture

of positivity, collaboration, and innovation.

15 LEADING THE CULTURE CHANGE

Leadership is a powerful tool used to guide people in their everyday lives, and it is especially valuable in a business setting. A leader is a figurehead who helps set the tone and vision for a company or organization. They are responsible for leading their team to reach their goals and objectives, while also inspiring and motivating them to reach their highest potential. Leaders must lead by example and be a role model for the people in their organization.

Leadership is about more than just setting goals and making decisions. It is about creating an environment that encourages growth, innovation, and success. A leader must also be able to bring out the best in their people by providing direction and motivation. They must be willing to take risks and challenge the status quo when necessary. It is also important for leaders to be open-minded, recognize mistakes, and be willing to make changes to improve the organization.

Leadership often involves change. It can be hard to get people to accept change, especially when it involves a shift in the culture or processes. It is essential that leaders have a clear vision of what they want to achieve and communicate this effectively to their team. They must also be willing to listen to feedback and adjust when necessary. Leaders should not be afraid to take risks, but they should also be aware that change can be difficult for people to understand and accept.

Leaders must also set a good example for their team. They should be punctual, professional, organized, and reliable. They should also be fair and treat everyone with respect. Leaders should be open and honest with their team and create a work environment where everyone feels valued and respected. A leader should also be available to answer questions and provide support when needed.

Leadership is an ongoing process. It requires continuous effort and dedication. Leaders should constantly strive to improve and push their team to excel. They should also be willing to adjust their approach, when necessary, in order to stay current and relevant. A leader must be committed to their team and must be willing to stay the course and not give up.

Culture is hard to change, and people will often be resistant to new ideas or processes. It is essential that leaders have a clear vision and understand what culture they want to create for their organization. They should also be aware of their team's strengths and weaknesses and try to create an environment that supports and encourages those strengths. Leaders must be patient and understanding and be willing to take the time to explain the new processes to their team and help them adjust to the changes.

Leaders should also be willing to invest in their team. They should provide them with the tools, resources, and training that are necessary to help them succeed. Leaders should also recognize and reward their team's hard work and accomplishments. This will give them a sense of purpose and help motivate them to do their best.

Leaders have the power to create a lasting impact on their

team, organization, and even the world. If they can lead by example, create an environment that encourages growth, and stay the course despite challenges, they can change the world and make it a better place. People will be happier, more productive, and more successful.

Leadership is not a one-time event, but rather an ongoing process. It requires constant effort and commitment. Leaders must be willing to take risks, challenge the status quo, and adjust when necessary. They must also be patient and understanding, while also recognizing and rewarding their team's hard work. If leaders can set the tone and provide the tools and resources to help their team reach their goals, they can truly make a lasting impact on their organization and the world.

16 BE THE LEADER YOU WANTED

As we all progress through our careers we will meet great leaders and some leaders that teach us what not to do. It is important to always realize that we have a responsibility to the people that we lead. We must be better than our predecessors and we have the opportunity to change leadership as it is currently known.

As we ascend the ladder of success, it is essential to not only meet exemplary leaders but also those who represent what leadership should not be. Leaders influence those around them and have the power to shape the future of an organization, a community, and even the nation. It is our responsibility to ensure that this power is used for good, and not for evil. We must rise to the challenge and take charge of our own lives, setting a new standard for leadership.

Leadership is not easy, and it requires courage, strength and conviction. We must have the courage to make difficult decisions, the strength to follow through, and the conviction to stay true to our values. We must embrace failure, learn from our mistakes, and continue to strive for excellence. We must also be aware of our own limitations and seek out mentors who can help us reach our goals. Without guidance and support, it is impossible to be successful in any role.

The most successful leaders are those who lead with integrity and humility. Integrity means that we are honest and ethical in all our dealings. Humility means that we recognize our strengths and weaknesses and are constantly looking for ways to improve. Successful leaders understand that leadership is not about status and power, but rather about serving and inspiring others. They recognize that it is their responsibility to create an environment where everyone can thrive.

Leadership also involves the ability to motivate and inspire those around us. We must be able to recognize people's strengths and weaknesses, challenge them to do their best, and foster a culture of collaboration and support. We must be brave, imaginative and creative in our approach, and use our skills to develop a vision of success.

Leadership also involves collaboration and teamwork. We must be able to recognize and engage with the strengths and weaknesses of those around us. We must use our skills to create an environment of trust and respect, where everyone feels valued and appreciated. We must be able to listen to and understand others, and be willing to compromise and make decisions that best serve the team.

We, as leaders, must take responsibility for our actions. We must be willing to accept criticism, learn from our mistakes and strive to be better. We must use our failures as a platform for growth and take ownership of our successes. We must be humble, resilient and never give up.

Never give up!

Culture change is hard, Changing an environment is just as hard. There will be set backs, and there will be times that you think you are not making progress. It is in these times that I remember a simple boxing match that taught me resilience at an early age. It is fitting to end with a story of resilience and determination. No matter how hard the fight seems and no matter how impossible it seems to change, it is possible. My hope with this book is to serve as the roadmap for others to change like I have seen possible.

In the early hours of February 11th, 1990, a boxing match between Mike Tyson and Buster Douglas was about to take place. The two fighters had made their way to the ring, ready to prove themselves and see who was the real champion of the heavyweight division. However, no one expected what was about to happen and it would become one of the most historic fights in boxing history.

The fight seemed to be in Tyson's favor right from the start. He had an undefeated record of 37-0, with 33 of his wins being by knockout. He was the undisputed heavyweight champion and was widely viewed by many as the greatest boxer of all time. In comparison, Buster Douglas had a much less impressive record, with only 29 wins and 4 losses. He was considered an underdog and many people felt he had no chance against "Iron" Mike Tyson.

When the fight started, the odds were definitely in Tyson's favor. He had a strong start and looked to be on the path to another victory. However, things quickly changed in the 8th round. Douglas managed to knock Tyson down and the champion was unable to get back up before the count of ten. This was a huge shock to everyone, including Tyson himself. It was now clear that the fight was anyone's game and that Douglas had a real chance of winning.

In the 10th round, Douglas was able to knock Tyson down yet again, this time for good, and the referee stopped the fight. The final result was that Buster Douglas had won the fight and had become the new undisputed heavyweight champion of the world. It was a huge upset, with the odds of Douglas winning the fight being estimated at 42-1.

When asked why he thought he won the fight, Buster Douglas

responded that he was fighting for his mother. It was later found out that his mother had told people that her son would beat Mike Tyson. Douglas' mother died 3 days before the fight. Buster Douglas won the fight because his "Why" was bigger than the punches he had to sustain. The victory of Buster Douglas would go on to have far-reaching implications. On that day, he showed the world that it was possible to beat Tyson, someone who had been deemed unbeatable. It inspired many people to believe in themselves and that anything is possible with hard work and dedication. The fight also showed that no one is unbeatable, no matter how great they may seem.

The fight between Tyson and Douglas also showed the world that no matter how hard the odds may be stacked against you, it is still possible to make your dreams come true. The story of Douglas showed that if you have the drive and determination, you can overcome any obstacle and come out victorious. It is a message that many have come to accept and has been spread around the world.

Resources

Maxwell, J. C. (2007). The 21 irrefutable laws of leadership. Thomas Nelson.

Rogers Everett, M. (1995). Diffusion of innovations. New York, 12.

ABOUT THE AUTHOR

Paul Hylenski is an Aerospace Composites Manufacturing Operations leader who works in Middle River, MD.

Paul started his leadership journey in the Marine Corps. He served as a Helicopter mechanic during his time in the Marines. He served at HMX-1 the Presidential Helicopter Squadron during his time of service.

For the past 15 years, he has worked on multiple different aerospace product lines, managing both the Assembly and Composite fabrication sections of the business. Additionally, he worked as a Six Sigma Blackbelt for the business, focusing on reducing defects and improving output.

Paul is passionate about Leadership because he feels, as leaders, we have the greatest responsibility to be able to make our team's lives better and help them to grow in their career. He has spent his business career changing culture by implementing psychological safety into aerospace manufacturing.

Paul has authored multiple articles about human-centric leadership and has a newsletter on LinkedIn dedicated to the subject.

Made in the USA
Middletown, DE
01 November 2023

41685887R00076